Pre-K

Preschool Skills

Ready for School

Illustrations by **Hector Borlasca**

FlashKids

An imprint of Sterling Children's Books

FLASH KIDS, STERLING, and the distinctive Sterling logo are registered trademarks of
Sterling Publishing Co., Inc.

Published by Sterling Publishing Co., Inc.
387 Park Avenue South, New York, NY 10016
Text and illustrations © 2005 by Flash Kids
Distributed in Canada by Sterling Publishing
c/o Canadian Manda Group, 165 Dufferin Street
Toronto, Ontario, Canada M6K 3H6
Distributed in the United Kingdom by GMC Distribution Services
Castle Place, 166 High Street, Lewes, East Sussex, England BN7 1XU
Distributed in Australia by Capricorn Link (Australia) Pty. Ltd.
P.O. Box 704, Windsor, NSW 2756, Australia

Sterling ISBN 978-1-4114-3425-7

Manufactured in Canada

Lot #:
21 23 25 24 22
01/17

For information about custom editions, special sales, premium and
corporate purchases, please contact Sterling Special Sales
Department at 800-805-5489 or specialsales@sterlingpublishing.com.

Cover illustrations, design, and production by Mada Design, Inc.

Dear Parent,

Help your child build a solid foundation for early learning with this Preschool Skills workbook. Colorful illustrations and fun activities introduce basic numbers, shapes, and colors, as well as key concepts such as opposites, attributes, and patterning. Your child will enjoy completing matching activities, finding hidden pictures, and learning to group similar objects based on size, shape, or common characteristics. Help your child make the most of this workbook with these tips:

- Provide a quiet, comfortable place for your child to complete this workbook. Go through each page with him or her slowly to ensure full comprehension of each activity.

- If your child answers a question incorrectly, explain why it is incorrect and allow your child to correct the mistake.

- Encourage your child to ask questions and have discussions about the things your child finds interesting in this book. You can also ask your child questions to keep him or her engaged in learning.

- Try to relate concepts found in this book to things your child encounters in everyday life. For example, have your child count toys as he or she puts them in a box, or ask your child to name the color or shape of common household items.

- Most of all, enjoy this special time spent together! Reading to your child and helping him or her learn will build a strong bond between you both.

This is red.

Strawberries are red.
Fire trucks are red.
Color the roses red.

This is orange.

ORANGE

Pumpkins are orange.
Oranges are orange.
Color the cat orange.

This is yellow.

Daffodils are yellow.
The sun is yellow.
Color the lemonade and
lemons yellow.

This is green.

Grass is green.
Frogs are green.
Color the turtle green.

This is blue.

The sky is blue.
Blueberries are blue.
Color the whale blue.

This is purple.

PURPLE

Grapes are purple.
Plums are purple.
Color the car purple.

Rainbow

A rainbow has many colors, including red, orange, yellow, green, blue, and purple. Use all the colors of the rainbow to color the picture below.

Up, Up, and Away!

Use the key to color the picture.

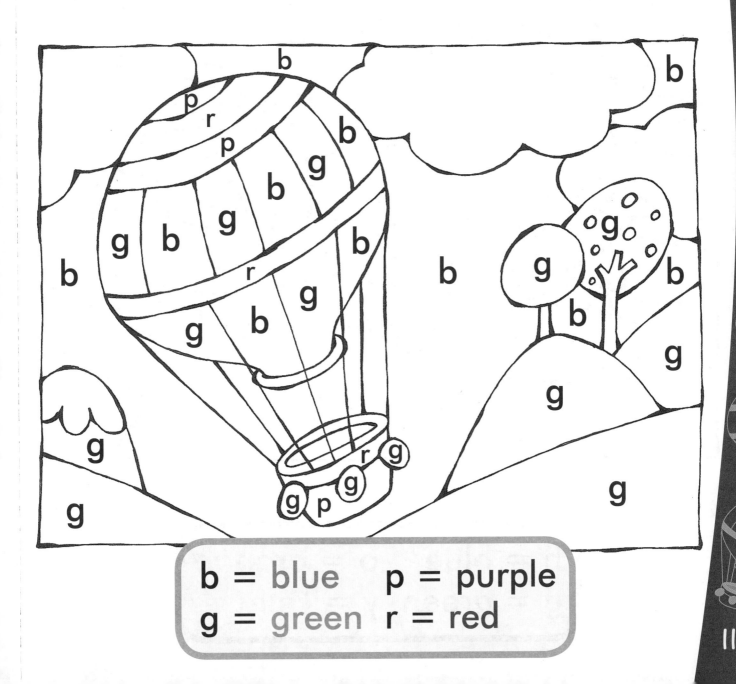

b = blue   p = purple
g = green   r = red

Under the Sea

Use the key to color the picture.

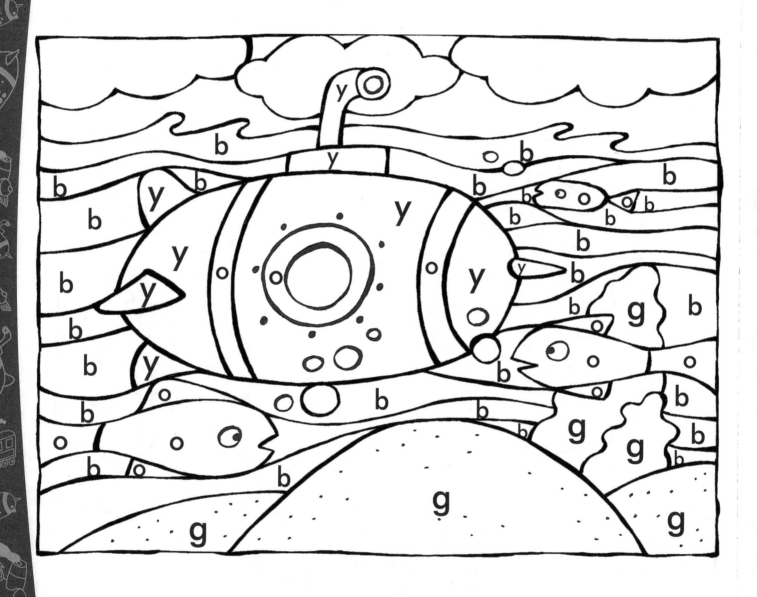

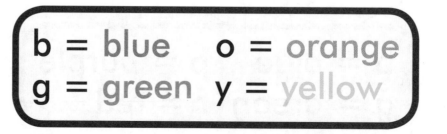

b = blue   o = orange
g = green   y = yellow

Choo Choo!

Use the key to color the picture.

b = blue   g = green
r = red   y = yellow

This is a circle.

A circle is round.
It has no corners.

Find and color the circles
in the picture.

This is a square.

A square has four corners. All four sides are the same size.

Find and color the squares in the picture.

This is a triangle.

A triangle has three sides. A triangle also has three corners.

Find and color the triangles in the picture.

This is a rectangle.

A rectangle has four sides. Two sides are long and two sides are short. A rectangle also has four corners.

Find and color the rectangles in the picture.

This is a heart.

Find and color the hearts in the picture.

This is a star.

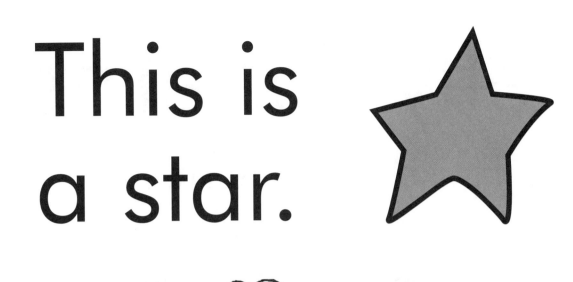

Find and color the stars
in the picture.

Pretty Patterns

Finish the patterns.

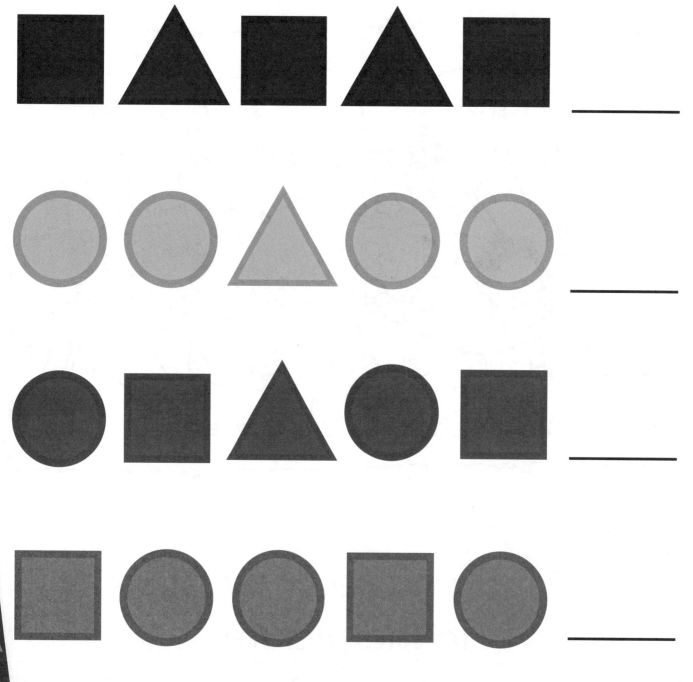

Shape Up

Finish the patterns.

What Comes Next?

Finish the patterns.

  _____ _____ _____ _____

   _____ _____

   _____ _____

Make Your Own!

Using the lines below, make your own patterns.

_____ _____ _____ _____

_____ _____ _____ _____

_____ _____ _____ _____

_____ _____ _____ _____

Pizza Match-Up

Draw a line between each item and its matching shape.

Twinkle, Twinkle

Draw a line between each item and its matching shape.

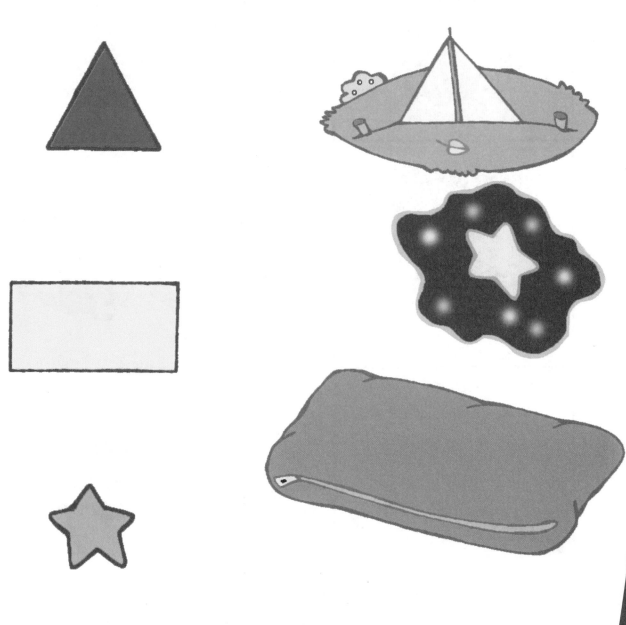

Same Size

Circle the picture that is the same size as the first.

Super Sizes

Draw a line between balls
of the same size.

Animal Match-up

Draw a line between each animal and its parent.

Where Do We Live?

Draw a line between each creature and its home.

Let's Get Dressed

Draw a line between things that belong together.

Around the House

Draw a line between things that belong together.

What a Pair

Circle the thing in each row that belongs with the first one.

We Belong

Circle the thing in each row that belongs with the first one.

Same or Different?

Cross out the thing in each row that doesn't belong.

Which Doesn't Belong?

Cross out the thing in each row that doesn't belong.

One

There is one tree.
Count the tree.

Practice writing the number 1.

1   1   1

Now draw one tree in the box.

Two

There are two kites.
Count the kites.

Practice writing the number 2.

2 2 2

Now draw two kites in the box.

Three

There are three clouds.
Count the clouds.

Practice writing the number 3.

3 3 3

Now draw three clouds in the box.

Four

There are four flowers.
Count the flowers.

Practice writing the number 4.

4 4 4

Now draw four flowers in the box.

Five

There are five butterflies.
Count the butterflies.

Practice writing the number 5.

5 5 5

Now draw five butterflies in the box.

Six

There are six balloons. Count the balloons.

Practice writing the number 6.

6 6 6

Now draw six balloons in the box.

Seven

There are seven balls.
Count the balls.

Practice writing the number 7.

7 7 7

Now draw seven balls in the box.

Eight

There are eight ladybugs.
Count the ladybugs.

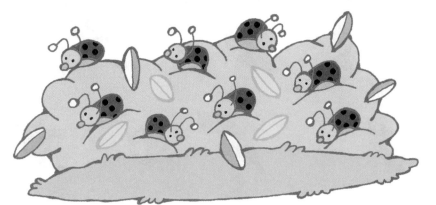

Practice writing the number 8.

8   8   8

Now draw eight ladybugs in the box.

Nine

There are nine leaves.
Count the leaves.

Practice writing the number 9.

9   9   9 — — — — — — —

Now draw nine leaves in the box.

Ten

There are ten stars. Count the stars.

Practice writing the number 10.

10 10 10 -- -- -- --

Now draw ten stars in the box.

Count the Critters

Count the animals in each row.
Circle the correct number.

2   3   4

3   4   5

2   4   6

1   3   5

Fun with Fish

Count the fish in each row.
Circle the correct number.

4	5	6
6	7	8
6	8	10
5	7	9

Bunches of Balls

Circle the group that has more.

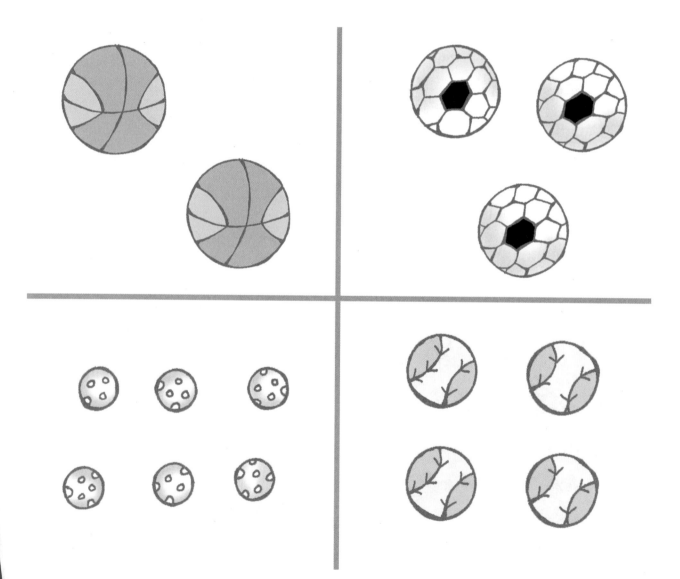

Lots of Leaves

Circle the group that has more.

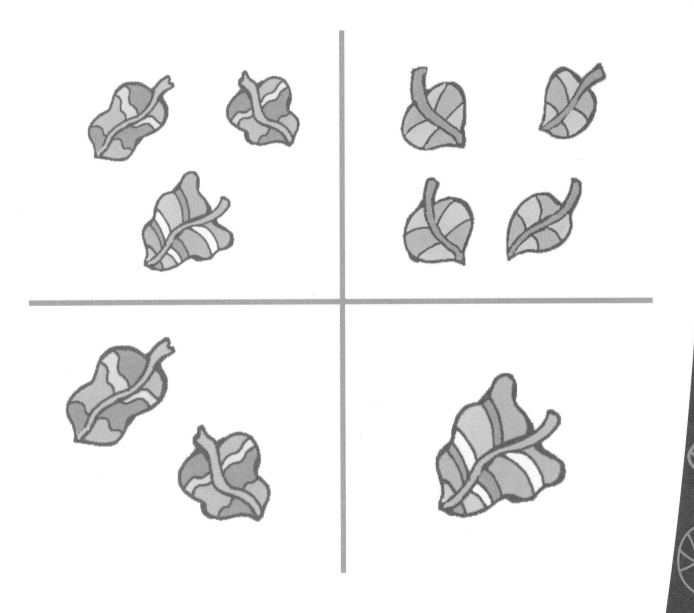

Fruit
Fun

Circle the group that has less.

More or Less

Circle the group that has less.

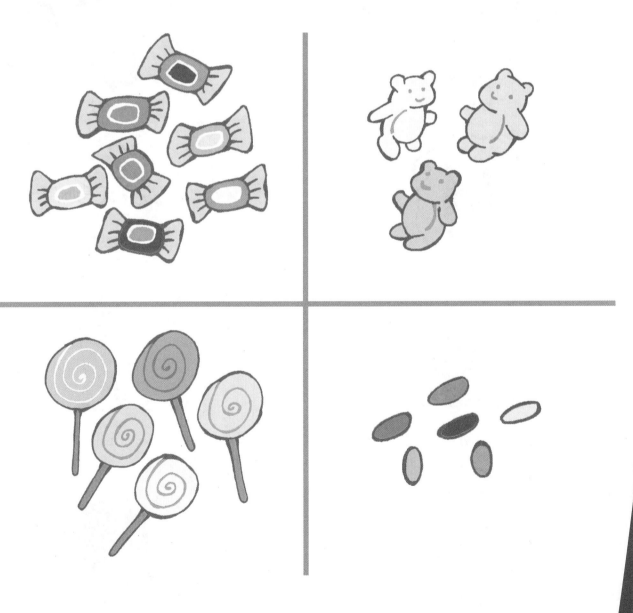

Opposites

Draw a line between each picture and its opposite.

happy

sad

closed

fast

full

slow

empty

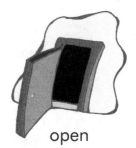

open

Opposites

Draw a line between each picture and its opposite.

young

dirty

hot

small

big

old

clean

cold

Rhyme Time!
Draw a line between words that rhyme.

dish

wig

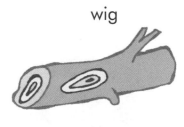

cat

log

dog

hat

pig

fish

More Rhymes!

Draw a line between words that rhyme.

house

cake

vest

coat

boat

nest

snake

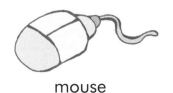

mouse

Rhyming Rows

Circle the word in each row that rhymes with the first one.

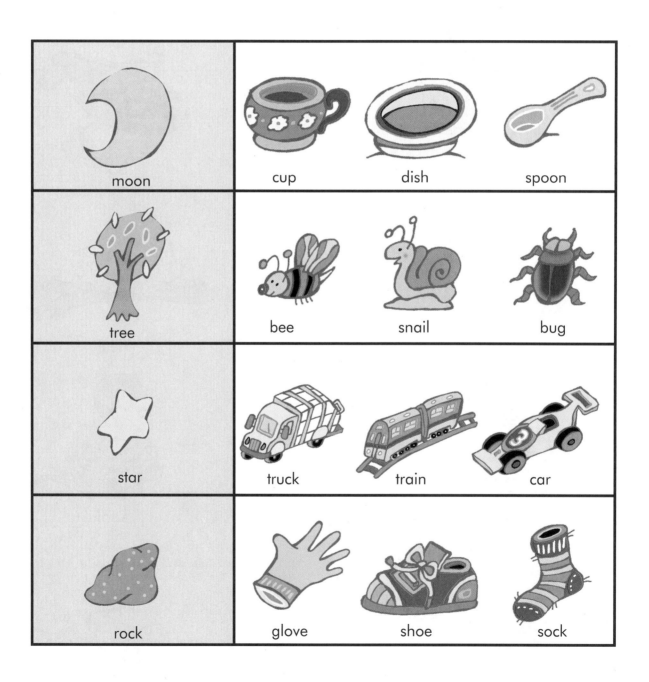

moon	cup	dish	spoon
tree	bee	snail	bug
star	truck	train	car
rock	glove	shoe	sock

Prime Rhymes

Circle the word in each row
that rhymes with the first one.

pie	eye	hand	foot
cake	mop	broom	rake
bread	chair	bed	table
fruits	suit	hat	umbrella

Animal Sounds

Draw a line between animals whose names have the same beginning sound.

dog

fish

fox

koala

bird

deer

kangaroo

bear

Animal Sounds

Draw a line between animals whose names have the same beginning sound.

horse

raccoon

alligator

hippo

rabbit

mouse

monkey

ant

Beginning Sounds

Circle the thing in each row that begins with the same sound as the first one.

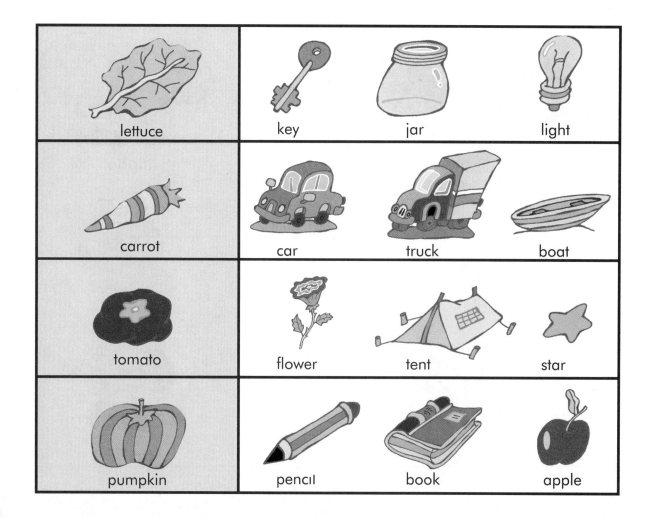

lettuce	key	jar	light
carrot	car	truck	boat
tomato	flower	tent	star
pumpkin	pencil	book	apple

More Sounds

Circle the thing in each row that begins with the same sound as the first one.

doll	duck	fox	bear
ball	apple	orange	banana
train	tree	flower	gate
jacks	jaguar	elephant	zebra

Uppercase Alphabet

Practice writing the uppercase alphabet.

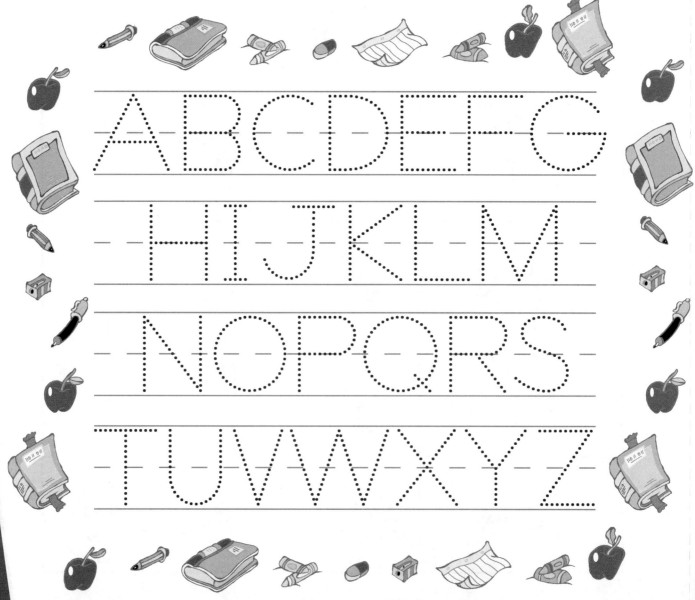

Lowercase Alphabet

Practice writing the lowercase alphabet.

a b c d e f g

h i j k l m n

o p q r s t u

v w x y z

Congratulations,

_____!
(Name)

You are ready
for school.